How God Guides Us

By Don Basham

True and False Prophets
The Most Dangerous Game
A Manual for Spiritual Warfare
How God Guides Us

HOW GOD GUIDES US

Don W. Basham

Manna Christian Outreach
Greensburg, Pennsylvania

Scripture quotations in this volume are from the King James Version of the Bible.

ISBN 0-8007-8199-6
Copyright © 1975 by Don W. Basham
Published by Manna Christian Outreach
All Rights Reserved
Library of Congress Catalog Card Number: 75-7145
Printed in the United States of America

Contents

Introduction

Although there are millions of Spirit-baptized Christians in America today, relatively few of them feel consistently led by the Holy Spirit. In traveling and teaching around the country, I encounter Christians everywhere who say to me, "Reverend Basham, I love the Lord and I want to serve Him faithfully. But how can I know what He wants me to do or where He wants me to go? If I feel led to do a certain thing, how can I be sure it's not my own desire or even the devil? *How can I be sure it's God?*"

Even mature Christians sometimes mistake their own desires for the will of God and all of us at times have been duped by Satan into foolish decisions and hasty actions. But, in *How God Guides Us*, it is not so much our desire to discuss the carnal nature or the wiles of Satan as to provide valid counsel for the myriads of Christians frozen in inactivity for fear of "missing God."

To discover how God guides us, we want to examine a portion of Scripture, in Acts chapters 15 and 16, which records one of the missionary journeys of Paul. In the process, we'll illustrate

four major principles in receiving and following
God's guidance. Here they are:

1   All progress in the Christian life is by
     faith.

2   Guidance comes when we move in
     faith, not when we sit in doubt.

3   God has a goal for each venture we
     undertake for Him.

4   Where God guides, He provides.

How God Guides Us

1

All Progress in the Christian Life Is by Faith

The often-asked question, "How can I be sure it's God?" reveals the most common misunderstanding of how God guides us: we expect to be *sure* of God's leading. But there is a basic contradiction between "being sure" and "having faith." "Being sure" eliminates the need for faith, and faith is indispensable to the Christian life.

> But without faith it is impossible to please him: for he that cometh to God must believe that he is, and that he is a rewarder of them that diligently seek him.
>
> Hebrews 11:6

Most Christians don't want to walk by faith, they want to walk by *certainty*. But God has ordained that we walk by *faith*, not by certainty. When people say to me, "But I'm not sure what God wants me to do," I reply, "Friend, if you could be sure, it wouldn't take any faith. God will not let you be 100 percent sure."

This means that, while God *will* guide us, normally His guidance is not so explicit or detailed that we don't have to exercise faith in following it. As I understand the essence of guidance, it consists of receiving subtle impressions from God, then, in faith, acting on those impressions trusting that they are from God.

God directs us by dropping His thoughts into the midst of our own—not by thundering in our ears or striking us with heavenly lightning. Our Scripture passage will clearly illustrate this truth.

Before we examine our text, let's first recognize a major problem we have in applying Scripture to our own lives. Because we tend to view the Bible and its heroes through 2,000 years of "stained-glass" history, we regard biblical characters as larger-than-life. We call them "Saint" John and "Saint" Paul. We name our cities, churches, and children after them. We gaze in awe at the works of master artists who portrayed them with haloes over their heads, and inwardly we think, "God's dealings with those men must have been unique." In a word, we regard Peter,

Paul, the disciples, and other heroes of the faith as "supersaints."

If we are to understand God's dealings with us, we must correct that distorted view. The apostles were ordinary people like us. They endured the same temptations and struggled against the same rebellious natures. They were saved by the grace of Jesus Christ just as we are, and were empowered and led by the same Holy Spirit who wants to empower and lead us in the same dynamic way. Perhaps the first verses in our Scripture passage may help us get rid of the halos over our supersaints.

Problems Among the Apostles

Chapter 15 of Acts begins with the Jerusalem conference of apostles and elders which met to decide whether Gentile Christians were required to keep the Law. When they agreed on certain restrictions the Gentile Christians should observe so as not to offend Jewish Christians, Paul proposed a return visit to the churches he and Barnabas had established to deliver the decision of the council and see how the churches were getting along. Barnabas wanted to take along John Mark, but Paul refused.

And some days after Paul said unto Barnabas,
Let us go again and visit our brethren in
every city where we have preached the word
of the Lord, and see how they do.

And Barnabas determined to take with them
John, whose surname was Mark.

But Paul thought not good to take him with
them, who departed from them from Pam-
phylia, and went not with them to the work.

Acts 15:36-38

Checking back in Acts 13:13, we discover
that on a previous missionary journey, John
Mark, apparently without Paul's approval, deserted the team and returned to Jerusalem.
Although no critical statement is made about his
leaving at the time, when Barnabas suggested
that they take Mark along on this trip, Paul
said in effect, "No, he deserted us before, and
I won't have a quitter along this time." A bitter,
angry dispute was the result.

And the contention was so sharp between
them, that they departed asunder one from
the other: and so Barnabas took Mark, and
sailed unto Cyprus;

And Paul chose Silas, and departed, being recommended by the brethren unto the grace of God.

And he went through Syria and Cilicia, confirming the churches.

Acts 15:39-41

I appreciate the frankness of the Scriptures. "The contention was so sharp . . . that they departed asunder." In other words, they had a knock-down-and-drag-out *church fight* right there in the "Antioch Missionary Society." Paul and Barnabas, spiritual giants of their own time, practically came to blows!

So much for the halos.

I find it encouraging when the Bible reveals the shortcomings of the leaders in the Early Church. I admire those men and do not mean to belittle them, but I thank God for the honesty of the Scriptures in showing that they also had their problems. That God used them mightily anyway gives me encouragement since it means God can use me, even with my problems.

The disagreement was so fierce that reconciliation was impossible. Barnabas and Paul went their separate ways—Barnabas with Mark, and

Paul with Silas. It is worth noting, incidentally, that Paul and Silas were "recommended by the brethren unto the grace of God," clearly indicating that they were ordained and commissioned for this trip. In light of our current awareness of principles of spiritual authority and the importance of being sent out by recognized leaders who stand responsible for the ministries they endorse, it's more than a little significant that Paul and Silas went with the blessing of the brethren. Apparently, Barnabas and Mark went without a similar recommendation.

Note also that up to this point there's nothing "superspiritual" about their trip. No voice of God thundering, no detailed revelation of God's "Master Plan." Paul simply suggested, "Let's go visit the churches," and he and Silas moved out. Now comes the second principle.

2

Guidance Comes When We Move in Faith, Not When We Sit in Doubt

Almost as soon as the journey got underway, the men ran into trouble.

And as they went through the cities, they delivered them the decrees for to keep, that were ordained of the apostles and elders which were at Jerusalem.

And so were the churches established in the faith, and increased in number daily.

Now when they had gone throughout Phrygia and the region of Galatia, and were forbidden of the Holy Ghost to preach the word in Asia. . . .

Acts 16:4-6

Paul and Silas started their trip, and picking up Timothy, traveled through Phrygia and Galatia, intending then to head over into Asia. I'm sure they sought God in this matter and thought they knew what He wanted them to

do. But apparently they headed in the wrong
direction, because the Holy Ghost slammed the
door in their faces. Dare we say it? They made
a mistake; *they missed their guidance*!

How God revealed their mistake doesn't
matter. Maybe they missed a boat or perhaps
someone sprained an ankle. The fact is, they
tried to go where the Lord didn't want them
to go, and He stopped them. So they tried again.

After they were come to Mysia, they assayed
[attempted] to go into Bithynia, but the
Spirit suffered them not.

Acts 16:7

When God prevented them from preaching
in Asia, they decided to go over into Bithynia.
But again, the Holy Ghost stood in the way,
blocking their entry into Bithynia. Dare we
say it again? *They missed their guidance a
second time*! Again, we don't know how it came
about; only that they wanted—even attempted
—to go, but God slammed another door in their
faces.

A most unexpected and humbling picture begins to emerge. Saint Paul, renowned missionary

and apostle extraordinaire, who had met Jesus face-to-face on the road to Damascus and later received revelations from the third heaven too sacred to share—this Spirit-filled, gift-endowed, number one leader of the Early Church finds himself, on this occasion, reduced to getting his guidance by ricocheting off doors slammed in his face by the Holy Ghost!

Not a very spiritual picture, you say? Not very supernatural? Right! Nevertheless, *closed doors are a valid part of guidance*. Actually, this should encourage rather than disturb us. It's as if God is saying, "Don't be afraid to move out. Don't be afraid of closed doors!"

I believe the story of Paul and Silas is in the Bible to help people like you and me. Most of us, when we bump against a closed door, sit dejectedly on that doorsill, wondering where we failed. The fear of failure paralyzes many modern Christians. Paul and Silas weren't daunted by the closed doors, they just sought God more earnestly. They realized that when God closes a door, it's because His plan involves something else. If He closes one door, He'll open another.

Years ago, while still in seminary in Oklahoma, I felt the urge to change universities. I applied for admission and was accepted by a fine sem-

inary in the state of Maryland. My wife and
I had once lived in Maryland and loved that
beautiful state. Besides, I thought it would be
"theologically broadening" to have training from
more than one seminary. But as the semester
drew to a close and we tried to prepare for our
move, nothing seemed to go right. Even routine
preparations seemed vastly complicated. And
the nearer the time came, the gloomier we felt.
Finally we decided God was telling us not to
move, and with a mixture of relief and disap-
pointment I reregistered for my next semester's
courses. Months later I discovered that by making a slight adjustment in my schedule, I could
complete the requirements for my graduate degree a whole semester earlier than I had antic-
ipated, something which would have been
impossible if we had changed schools. My wife
and I ended up praising God for the door He
had closed in our faces.

Guidance can only come when we continue
to move in faith, even in the face of the closed
doors. Remember, closed doors are an inevitable
part of every Christian's life; they are signposts
pointing toward other, *open* doors.

The guidance we are describing is like the
rudder on a ship. The rudder functions only

when the ship is moving. Just after we moved to
Florida some years ago, the *Queen Elizabeth*
was retired from ocean-going service and berthed
at Port Everglades in Ft. Lauderdale. Driving
by the ship as she rested high in the water, we
could see at her stern the huge rudder which
had steered that great vessel safely across the
Atlantic on hundreds of voyages. But as long
as the *Queen Elizabeth* rested in that harbor,
the rudder never did a thing. It wasn't needed
because the ship wasn't moving. That's how
it is with the guidance we seek. It may never
come until we trust God enough to start moving
in faith. Then His guidance comes—like a course
correction—when necessary. God may close some
doors which beckon attractively. If He does,
it's because the door of His choosing is open
further down the line. Don't be afraid of closed
doors!

In the case of our Scripture story, the doors
God closed led to an open door in Macedonia,
for on their third attempt to find God's direction, God gave Paul a vision of a man from
Macedonia saying, "Come over and help us."
(By the way, that man in the vision is significant,
as we'll see further on in the story.) Convinced
now that they have the correct guidance, the

missionary team embarked for Macedonia (see
Acts 16:10).

Isn't it interesting that God didn't give Paul
that vision before he began the trip? He had
to move out in faith and bump into those closed
doors; *then* God gave the vision. But notice:
even then, *He gave only enough information to
get them headed in the right direction.*

Finally, an Open Door

And a vision appeared to Paul in the night;
There stood a man of Macedonia, and prayed
him, saying, Come over into Macedonia, and
help us.

And after he had seen the vision, immediately
we endeavoured to go into Macedonia, as-
suredly gathering that the Lord had called us
for to preach the gospel unto them.

Therefore loosing from Troas, we came with a
straight course to Samothracia, and the next
day to Neapolis;

And from thence to Philippi, which is the
chief city of that part of Macedonia, and a
colony: and we were in that city abiding certain days.

And on the sabbath we went out of the city by a river side, where prayer was wont to be made; and we sat down, and spake unto the women which resorted thither.

And a certain woman named Lydia, a seller of purple, of the city of Thyatira, which worshipped God, heard us: whose heart the Lord opened, that she attended unto the things which were spoken of Paul.

And when she was baptized, and her household, she besought us, saying, If ye have judged me to be faithful to the Lord, come into my house, and abide there. And she constrained us.

Acts 16:9-15

At last, it appeared that everything had fallen into proper order for the missionary team. After closing one door, and then another, God gave Paul a vision. They were needed in Macedonia. Luke, the author of Acts, joined them in verse 10, indicated by the change in pronoun from "they" to "we." Up to this point, he had been recounting the details as history, but now he became part of the tour. (It's very interesting,

also, the points at which Luke says "we" and
the points at which it's "they." When things
get tough later on, Luke suddenly "lets himself
out" of a rugged situation by simply reverting
to "they" in his narrative.)

Paul, Silas, Timothy, and Luke boarded a ship
to Philippi, a major city in Macedonia, and
immediately on arriving, found a small prayer
meeting down by the riverside where they could
preach. Paul made a convert, a woman named
Lydia, who opened her home to them as a nice
little parsonage for their room and board.

So at last, things seemed to be working out.
After several false starts, the missionary tour
began to produce results. Not only had the
team revisited some of their established churches,
now they began a new one. They had a congregation to preach to, a parsonage which provided
them with room and board, and people were
being saved. How much more success could
they want?

However, this success was not what God had
in mind for their visit to Philippi, as we shall
quickly discover in our third principle.

3

God Has a Goal for Each Venture We Undertake for Him

As we examine the rest of the story, a significant fact emerges: the missionary team is moving in faith toward *their* goal, but *God* has another goal in mind for their journey. Although He hasn't informed Paul and Silas of His plan, we'll see as the story progresses that it's the very reason for those closed doors and other more drastic changes in their circumstances.

God often works in us the same way! He may send us someplace letting us think we're to do one thing, only to find when we arrive that He had something altogether different in mind. Like it or not, that's often God's way. He doesn't bother to tell us His full plan ahead of time, so long as we're moving in the right direction. He guides us just one step at a time.

I believe God most often withholds His long-range strategy from us for two reasons:

1   If we could see the victories which lie ahead, we'd get puffed up and prideful.

2   If we could see the problems which lie
       ahead, we'd become too fearful to go on.

Moving in faith means walking step by step.
The psalmist says, "Thy word is a lamp unto
my feet . . ." (Psalms 119:105), but most of us
would prefer a searchlight shining two miles
down the road. Like it or not, God reveals each
part of His plan as we walk in obedience *one
step at a time*. Little did Paul and Silas know
that the next step they were to take would
touch off a powder keg in Philippi.

The City Explodes

And it came to pass, as we went to prayer, a
certain damsel possessed with a spirit of div-
ination met us, which brought her masters
much gain by soothsaying:

The same followed Paul and us, and cried,
saying, These men are the servants of the most
high God, which shew unto us the way of
salvation.

And this she did many days. But Paul, being
grieved, turned and said to the spirit, I com-
mand thee in the name of Jesus Christ to

come out of her. And he came out the same
hour.

And when her masters saw that the hope of
their gains was gone, they caught Paul and
Silas, and drew them into the marketplace
unto the rulers,

And brought them to the magistrates, saying, These men, being Jews, do exceedingly
trouble our city,

And teach customs, which are not lawful for
us to receive, neither to observe, being Romans.

And the multitude rose up together against
them: and the magistrates rent off their
clothes, and commanded to beat them.

And when they had laid many stripes upon
them, they cast them into prison, charging
the jailor to keep them safely:

Who, having received such a charge, thrust
them into the inner prison, and made their
feet fast in the stocks.

Acts 16:16-24

Suddenly the team's successful ministry became a nightmare. In order to fulfill His plan,

God stepped back as it were, and allowed Satan to kick up a storm. On the way to the prayer meeting by the riverside, Paul cast the demon out of a fortune-telling slave girl, whose enraged owners had him and Silas arrested. Because Paul had ventured into the devil's territory (and this often happens when we challenge Satan on his own ground), all was chaos in that town. Suddenly, there was a city-wide insurrection.

Angered by the deliverance, Satan whipped the city courtroom into a frenzied mob so that the magistrates treated Paul and Silas, two unpretentious itinerant preachers, like public enemies number one and two. They were beaten by the magistrates and thrown, not just into prison, but into the *inner* prison.

In most prisons, there is an outer block of cells, then a corridor, then another inner block of cells where the maximum security prisoners are placed to make it doubly difficult for them to break out. Obviously, Paul and Silas were considered to be highly dangerous prisoners, since the jailer put them in that inner cell block. In addition, he fastened their feet in stocks, as if they literally were revolutionaries out to destroy the town. The charge given to the jailer was to keep them from escaping or it would cost him his life.

What a reversal of circumstances! Successful missionaries that morning, by midnight they had been arrested, beaten, and cast into prison.

Opposition From the Devil

If we examine the events following the arrest, there seems absolutely no justification for all that violent uproar over two itinerant preachers. But the whole incident blew sky-high in order that God's purposes might be served, as we shall see.

Suppose you were arrested for witnessing to your faith: how would you take it? I'm afraid most Christians today would immediately assume they were out of God's will because they ran into such difficulty. We live in such sheltered, comfortable circumstances that if our faith really begins to cost us something we assume we have missed God's guidance. We need to realize that just because opposition arises, it does not mean we have missed our guidance or that we are out of God's will. As a matter of fact, scripturally the verification of being *in* the will of God is opposition and harassment.

Yea, and all that will live godly in Christ
Jesus shall suffer persecution.

2 Timothy 3:12

Too frequently, when things get tough we
say, "Where did we go wrong? Why is everyone
mad at us?" Usually, we haven't done anything
wrong: *just walking in obedience* is enough to
incur the devil's wrath and have him raise an
uproar. Understand this: God knows it can
happen! He even sets up situations where it
will happen.

Look at the ministry of Jesus. After He was
baptized in the Jordan River by John, and the
Spirit descended upon Him like a dove, Scripture
says, "And Jesus . . . was led by the Spirit into
the wilderness, Being forty days tempted of the
devil . . ." (Luke 4:1,2). Who was it that set Him
up for that forty days of temptation? *The Holy
Spirit.* The devil didn't lure Him, God *led* Him
out there to meet His enemy face-to-face. Why?
Because God's will for Jesus—and for every
one of us—is that we confront the enemy face-
to-face. The only way we learn what our authority is in God is to have it challenged.

Opposition from the devil doesn't mean we've

missed God, since whatever the devil tries to do or actually does to us is allowed by God (*see* Job 1:8-12). In the long run, the devil is another instrument God can manipulate when necessary to get His will accomplished. This may sound rather strange, but we need to understand that even what the devil does is subject to God's jurisdiction.

Those of us in the deliverance ministry or in the healing ministry know that it is God's sovereign will for people to be set free and to be made whole. But in the permissive will of God, although He *knows* that sickness or oppression is an attack by the enemy, He will not always stop the enemy from attacking. God *has* made provision for our victory, and by confronting the enemy we learn what we are in Jesus Christ and how to *stand* and *assert* our authority. So God allows the devil to attack us, in the confidence that if we will apply the authority we have in Jesus, we'll come through with the victory. But notice that the word *victory* implies struggle, warfare, battle. Unless there's a battle, there can be no victory.

So even what the devil does, God allows. This is what happened to Paul and Silas. God stepped back and let the devil run wild, stirring up the whole town because, in the end, it was to serve His purposes.

Miracles in the Prison

And at midnight Paul and Silas prayed, and sang praises unto God: and the prisoners heard them.

And suddenly there was a great earthquake, so that the foundations of the prison were shaken: and immediately all the doors were opened, and every one's bands were loosed.

And the keeper of the prison awaking out of his sleep, and seeing the prison doors open, he drew out his sword, and would have killed himself, supposing that the prisoners had been fled.

But Paul cried with a loud voice, saying, Do thyself no harm: for we are all here.

Then he called for a light, and sprang in, and came trembling, and fell down before Paul and Silas,

And brought them out, and said, Sirs, what must I do to be saved?

And they said, Believe on the Lord Jesus
Christ, and thou shalt be saved, and thy house.

And they spake unto him the word of the
Lord, and to all that were in his house.

And he took them the same hour of the night,
and washed their stripes; and was baptized,
he and all his, straightway.

And when he had brought them into his house,
he set meat before them, and rejoiced, be-
lieving in God with all his house.

Acts 16:25-34

Many times, when difficult situations arise,
we begin to moan and complain. Fortunately,
the drastic change from preaching to prison did
not bring Paul and Silas to despair. Indeed,
they maintained the victory, even in jail.

In a contemporary situation, if any of us
ended up in jail with our feet in stocks and
backs raw and bleeding, we would probably complain to one another. Silas might well have said,
"Paul, why did you cast the demon out of that
girl? Couldn't you have just prayed a nice,
soothing prayer for her and let it go at that?
Look at all the trouble you've caused." But

Silas *didn't* complain, and neither did Paul. Hands and feet may have been fastened in stocks, but their spirits were still free! They were singing hymns, praising God, and testifying to the prisoners.

It's obvious from Paul's statements: "I know both how to be abased, and I know how to abound" (Philippians 4:12), and ". . . for I have learned, in whatsoever state I am, therewith to be content . . ." (Philippians 4:11), that he knew what it was to be driven right down into the dirt, and yet maintain the victory. Even when beaten and thrown in prison, Paul and Silas remained joyous and faithful to the Lord. And God honored their faith and punctuated their testimony to those prisoners with an earthquake. (How's that for "signs and wonders" attesting to the gospel?)

When the earthquake struck, the lights went out, the prison shook, the doors opened, and the stocks even fell off the prisoners. The jailer came rushing in from the next room, and seeing the cell doors open, he assumed everyone had escaped, and drew his sword to kill himself. But the same Holy Ghost who had opened the doors and stocks had also held the prisoners in place, and Paul shouted to him, "Don't do that—we're all still here."

Now, that jailer didn't have suicidal tendencies. In all likelihood, he would have been tortured to death for letting the prisoners escape, and he was going to save the authorities the trouble. But when Paul shouted, "We're all here," the jailer, astounded by the double miracle of the earthquake and the prisoners still sitting in their cells, fell on his face before them trembling and said, "Sirs, what must I do to be saved?"

His reaction poses an interesting question: how did he even know there was such a thing as salvation? He knew because Paul and Silas obviously weren't just singing hymns and praising God, they were preaching to the prisoners. The jailer had overheard their preaching, but remained unconvinced. However, when God punctuated the sermon with an earthquake, and when the jailer returned and found these men free, he thought, "This must be God," and he accepted Christ.

Now I believe that about this time, Paul must have taken a second look at this man and said, "Haven't I seen you somewhere before?" I believe the jailer was the man from Macedonia in the vision who said, "Come over and help us." Although I may not be able to prove it word for word, the whole weight of the Scripture implies that God had the jailer in mind the moment that missionary journey started.

God's Goal for the Journey

We said Paul and Silas were conducting the tour with one purpose in mind while God was sovereignly working toward another. As Paul and Silas moved in obedience to the first two principles—all progress in the Christian life is by faith and guidance comes when we move in faith, not when we sit in doubt—God was working His deeper plan in accordance with the third principle: God has a goal for each venture we undertake for Him. I believe it was His plan from the beginning of Paul's tour that the jailer and his household be converted, even though this purpose was not made known to Paul and Silas until after it had been fulfilled.

Why was this particular jailer so significant? Certainly, in God's unbiased regard for every man, he was no more important, no more loved than anyone else. Space does not permit a full discussion of why the jailer was so important to the Lord. It is sufficient to note that in the strategy of divine warfare, as in human warfare between nations, certain places, incidents, and people are strategic. I believe the jailer was such a strategic objective. At any rate, he was God's objective for *this* trip. In World War II, many little-known islands in the Pacific became historic battle sites. For example, Iwo Jima, just a hunk of volcanic coral with little intrinsic worth, was practically unheard of, and yet a major engagement was fought there between the United States and Japan. Why? Because it was a *strategic* place in the Pacific war. Similarly, people and incidents in Scripture are strategic in the heavenly warfare, and the conversion of the jailer and his household was somehow a key point in God's strategy. He had it in mind from the beginning.

Once we understand that it was God's will that the jailer and his household be converted, we can see the significance of the entire journey, and especially the closed doors. God had the jailer in mind when Paul said, "Let's go back and visit the churches." Although He did allow some of those churches to be visited, His more specific goal was the conversion of the jailer's household. When Paul and Barnabas blew up at each other and went their separate ways, this was still God's objective. And when Paul and

Silas started out, God made the necessary changes in their itinerary to accomplish His purpose.

When they tried to go into Asia, God slammed the door shut, because that jailer wasn't in Asia, he was in Philippi in Macedonia. And when they tried to go into Bithynia, God slammed *that* door. Why? Because the jailer wasn't in Bithynia, he was in Philippi.

Finally, God provided a vision to get the team headed in the right direction. They arrived in Philippi in Macedonia and began a successful ministry; the congregation by the riverside, the parsonage with room and board, and converts. But as nice as those blessings were, they did not fulfill God's *specific* purpose: He was out to win that jailer. And the jailer wasn't attending the prayer meetings by the riverside—*the jailer was in the jail*. So, in order to get the gospel to the jailer, God had to get the preachers in jail.

Because God wanted that jailer converted, He stepped back and allowed Satan to stir up a riot in the city court so Paul and Silas would be considered dangerous enough to be put into that maximum security cell; *right next* to the room where the jailer stayed.

Of course, at this point, God's strategy and eventual goal were still unknown to Paul and Silas. All they knew was that they were in plenty of trouble, and they resolved to simply endure the hardship for Christ's sake. So, without complaint, they said, "Well—Praise God, we've got a captive audience," and they began to testify and preach to the other prisoners. They had no way of knowing that the real target for their witnessing was not the prisoners but the jailer. But God knew this, because He had placed them in the only cell where the jailer couldn't help but overhear their testifying and preaching to the prisoners. And when God saw that the jailer remained unconvinced by what he heard, He punctuated their message with the earthquake.

With the miracle of the earthquake and the events immediately following it, the jailer had a change of heart. He fell before Paul and said, "Sirs, what must I do to be saved?" Once again, where had he heard the message of salvation? Listening to Paul preach to the prisoners. But isn't it strange to note that, so far as we know, not a single prisoner was converted? Only the jailer, who wasn't even a part of the audience. This is a graphic illustration of how God uses our walk in faith to accomplish, not what we want, but what He wants. That's why we are not to be afraid or downcast over closed doors or adverse circumstances. What may seem difficult or humiliating is often later revealed as God working out His greater purposes!

In this case, God's purpose for their stay in Philippi was fulfilled once the jailer and his household were saved. As we finish the story in the Scriptures, we'll see how this is true.

God Takes the Pressure Off

Previously, when Paul and Silas were thrown into prison as public enemies Number One and Two, the whole town had been in an uproar because of them. That was at midnight. Now let's pick up the story as it continues with verse 35 of chapter 16.

And when it was day, the magistrates sent the serjeants, saying, Let those men go.

Acts 16:35

"And when it was day. . . ." Just six hours after Paul and Silas were imprisoned, the magistrates had done a complete about-face. At midnight, they had been ready to put them to death or keep them in prison for life as public enemies Number One and Two. A mere six hours later, they had a complete change of heart for no explainable reason. Except *one*. God had accomplished what He wanted with those men in prison, so He took the pressure off. The sergeants and the magistrates probably said to one another, "What did we get so upset about? Why all the furor over two itinerant preachers and a slave girl? We don't really need to hold those men." So they sent for the sergeant and said, "Let those men go."

Paul Demands an Apology

And the keeper of the prison told this saying to Paul, The magistrates have sent to let you go: now therefore depart, and go in peace.

But Paul said unto them, They have beaten us openly uncondemned, being Romans, and have cast us into prison; and now do they thrust us out privily? nay verily; but let them come themselves and fetch us out.

Acts 16:36, 37

Here we see a little of Paul's thorny char-
acter. As this passage demonstrates, Paul was
not above throwing his weight around on occasion.
When the prison keeper came to release them,
Paul pulled himself up to his full "five-foot-five"
(tradition says he was small of stature) and
said to them, "They put us in here illegally—
now let them come and apologize." That certainly doesn't sound very spiritual of Paul does
it? Rather than just quietly leaving the prison,
he became indignant. "Those men were wrong
and they're going to have to come and apologize
for it."

Farewell to Prison and Philippi

And the serjeants told these words unto the
magistrates: and they feared, when they heard
that they were Romans.

And they came and besought them, and
brought them out, and desired them to depart
out of the city.

Acts 16:38, 39

Upon hearing Paul was a Roman citizen, the
magistrates panicked because they had no right
to throw them into prison. Paul asserted his

Roman citizenship more than once. He did it again before Festus and God used his appeal to Caesar to get him into Rome to preach the gospel (*see* Acts 25:10-12).

Anyway, the magistrates came back and let them go.

> And they went out of the prison, and entered into the house of Lydia: and when they had seen the brethren, they comforted them, and departed.
>
> Acts 16:40

Silas could well have said, "Praise God, He's delivered us by a miracle. Now let's go back to the riverside. Paul, what's your text for this sermon? I wonder what Lydia has fixed for lunch." But Paul and Silas, able now to recognize the sovereign working of God in their situation, knew that with the conversion of the jailer, their mission there was finished. They returned to Lydia's house and said, "Let's have a prayer— we're leaving." And they bade the brethren at Lydia's house good-bye and sailed away, their job in Philippi accomplished.

4

Where God Guides, He Provides

God has a goal for each venture we undertake for Him, and where God guides, He provides. Ironically, a part of His provision for Paul and Silas was getting them in jail. We don't like to think of God's provision in those terms, but we need to recognize that He supplies the tests as well as the blessings. God not only meets our needs to carry on the ministry He has for us, but He also allows adversity in order that the ministry may be what He wants it to be, and that's not always pleasant. The Lord allows such chastening to prune us—all for our own good and for the fulfillment of His purposes.

So these are the principles running through this story:

1   All progress in the Christian life is by faith.
2   Guidance comes when we move in faith, not when we sit in doubt. Like the rudder of a ship, guidance does not take effect until we begin to move. We must

step out in faith, realizing that if we start to make a mistake, God will be in a position to guide us. The rudder will take hold, and God will steer us in the direction that He desires.

3   God has a goal for each venture we undertake for Him. He has a plan for every period of our lives, and when we link up with God, all kinds of unpredictable things begin to happen—tests as well as blessings.

4   Where God guides, He provides.

I want to share some personal experiences along this line, because I'm not speaking through the top of my hat on this subject. I've *lived* this way for seven years, and I can testify that these principles are reliable and true.

Leaving Security Behind

A series of circumstances combined about seven years ago to lead me to resign from the pastorate. I had been a pastor for almost fifteen years when doors began to open to ministry outside my local church, primarily through the publication of my first book. As more and more

invitations to speak came, I began to feel that
God wanted me out of the institutional pastorate.
Of course, the problem I was immediately con-
fronted with was: how could I know that it
was really what God wanted me to do? I had
a career in the pastorate—a certain reputation—
a certain denominational standing—salary, parsonage, pension plan, car allowance, a month's
paid vacation. In a word, I had *security*.

Reluctantly, I would ask, "Now, God, You
want me to give all this up in order to step out
and become an itinerant preacher, on faith, with
no visible means of support, just to follow what
You want me to do?" It sounded exciting, but
practically speaking, it also sounded foolish. How
could I make a living? How would my wife and
five children be provided for?

I believed these principles: that there was no
progress in the Christian life except by faith,
and that God had a goal for my life. Yet I'd find
myself praying, "God, I think this is what You
want me to do, but show me—let me be *sure*.
This is a big step You're asking me to take.
Show me where I'll go, what I'll do, how I'll
be provided for." At the time, I was $2,500 in
debt, with a substantial car payment, and various
other outstanding bills. Our growing family was

just barely scrimping by as it was. I'd say, "Show me that this is Your will for me by giving me some sign. I don't want to miss Your guidance."

Every time, I'd get the same answer back from God in my spirit. Now, I don't hear a great thundering voice saying, "Thus saith the Lord, get in thine car, drive twelve blocks, turn right. . . ." Instead, whenever I would ask, "Lord, *show* me how it's all going to work out," the quiet inner voice of God would clearly reply, "Step out and *then* I'll show you." Guidance comes when we move in faith, not when we sit in doubt.

For years, I had preached from behind the security of my pulpit, "You can trust God. Where God guides, He provides." And I could preach sermons with illustrations taken from the life of George Mueller, the great English Christian who started the Bristol orphanages and prayed in over five million dollars in his lifetime without ever asking a soul for money. Recounting the miracles that flowed in response to his prayers, I would tell my people, "You could be like George Mueller—just pray it in. If God leads you to do something, *do it* in faith, because where God guides He provides."

Although I could preach that from behind the pulpit, I found it's another thing to step out and actually do it. Would my own advice work in my own case? I also found that if you believe a thing and proclaim it—*watch out*! Sooner or later, God will make you walk your words out in faith.

Finally I realized that I would have to obey or compromise my own preaching. Since God wouldn't show me anything more than He had already showed me, with a great burst of enthusiasm (or faith), I resigned. I called my church board together and said I was resigning and moving my family to Florida. I already knew some spiritual work was going on down there, and I wanted to situate my family in a relatively mild climate (just in case we had to live on the street).

There are many stories of God's provision connected with our stepping out in faith. One concerned the $2,500 debt that faced us. I couldn't see beginning a whole new ministry $2,500 in debt. Repeatedly I said, "God, give me $2,500 and let me start free of debt." Then God began to remind me that for years I had been putting money in my denominational pension fund toward my retirement. I knew that any time a man left the denomination, or wanted to cancel out of the plan, he could get back what he had invested. When God would remind me of this, I'd say, "But, Lord, that's for my retirement— for my old age. Surely You don't want me to tamper with that." Finally I saw the inconsistency of trusting God for the next thirty years, but then after that, relying on Social Security and my pension fund.

Seeing the inconsistency is one thing—doing something about it is something else. I still didn't want to cancel the pension fund. Yet, whenever I'd pray, "Lord, give me $2,500," I'd hear this little voice say, "Pension fund, pension fund." So I finally canceled out and got enough money to pay myself out of debt and move my family to Florida. But then, the school of faith started.

I hadn't been in Florida six weeks until God began to slam one door after the other, and within weeks, I was broke. With a wife and five children to support, that will put backbone into your praying.

Someone has described the life of faith this way: "Living by faith is like living in the midst of a miracle on the edge of disaster." That's how it is. If God doesn't come through, you go under!

Let me say first of all that seven years later,

I can testify that *God will not let you go under*. In all of these years, we have never suffered real need or gone hungry. Now, admittedly, my wife has fixed a few funny menus during the time, but we've never gone hungry, nor have we neglected any financial obligations. But we have been without money on any number of occasions. And this happened only a few weeks after we arrived in Florida.

The Broken Headlight

I had only twelve dollars one night when I went to bed, and I woke up the next morning with a sinking feeling. "Only twelve dollars, no invitations to speak, no other money in sight," I moaned to myself. Besides that, a headlight on our station wagon had burned out and I just woke up with the impression, "Go get the headlight fixed." That would surely take three or four dollars. I said, "Lord, I don't want to do that. Three or four dollars would buy hamburger to feed my family. Surely You wouldn't want me to spend that three or four dollars for the headlight." But the impression remained: "Get the headlight fixed," and I finally said, "Well, all right."

But even then, I wouldn't do it. Instead, I

fiddled around the house until Alice, my wife, said, "What's the matter with you anyway?" I mumbled, "Well, you know we're nearly broke."

"God's going to look after us," she replied.

"Yeah—well—maybe so, but He's told me to go get the headlight replaced. We only have twelve dollars and it'll take four dollars to do that."

Alice gave me a kiss and gently shoved me toward the door saying, "You go be obedient—who knows what you're holding up by not being obedient."

So I had the headlight replaced. It was like pulling skin off my arm to pay the man at the service station four dollars, but I returned home feeling a little better. As I came in the door, Alice was answering the phone.

"It's for you," she said. It was an invitation to speak at a prayer meeting in Hollywood, Florida that night. I thought, "Praise the Lord, they'll take up an offering." (Honestly, I was so relieved I never even considered what message I should give.)

Then the mail came a little later and with it two unexpected checks: one for $400 and one for $150. I received $50 in the meeting and went to bed that night with $600.

Even $600 doesn't last forever, and this sort

of situation would arise time and again. But God has been abundantly faithful, and has never let us go under.

There have been other occasions when His timing was almost unbelievable, and through such times, I discovered *where* your faith really grows. It grows between that time when you think God *has* to answer and that time when He finally *does* answer. We'd sweat it right out to the deadline, and I'd pray, "God, unless You do something, we're sunk!" and it was just like He'd say, "It's going to be all right." Then we would just be held in suspension, sometimes for days when we just didn't seem to need any cash. And finally, the needed money would come, just in time.

One time I was driving around in Ft. Lauderdale complaining because I was broke. I said, "Lord, You know I don't have any money."

And suddenly He said in my spirit, "What do you need that you don't have?" You know, I couldn't think of a thing! There was gas in the car, food in the refrigerator, my family was well clothed—and I had to laugh.

"Lord, I can't think of a thing. It's just that I don't like going around with no money in my pocket."

An Easter Present

God's provision wasn't always money. The
first Easter we were in Florida, our girls were
complaining to my wife at the lunch table. The
girls said, "Other kids are getting new dresses
for Easter, Mother. We want new dresses." At
the time, we didn't even have enough money
to windowshop.

Alice asked, "Have you prayed about it?",
and Shari Beth, our second daughter said, "Oh,
Mother!" All the girls were fussing and fuming,
but Alice persisted, "Well, you ought to pray
about it." We've taken our children into this
life of faith and had prayed with them before
in similar situations. I don't think we had even
left the table before a knock came at the door.

It was a delivery man with a gift-wrapped
package. Cindi, our oldest brought it to my wife,
and everyone became excited that somebody was
giving us a present. Alice opened it—it was a
white box full of tissue paper, but when she
pushed the paper around, it seemed that there
was nothing else in the box.

Lisa, our next-to-the-youngest, a little blue-
eyed blond, complained, "Mother, somebody's
playing a trick on us." But in the bottom of the

box, there was an envelope with a card in it. Alice read the card, and with tears in her eyes, handed it to me.

It was a gift certificate made out to a local women's clothing store in the amount of one hundred dollars. The kids began to jump up and down: "You mean we can have $100 worth of clothes *for free*?"

"That's what the card says," I replied.

My son Glenn, who had remained sagely quiet through all this talk about women's clothes, asked, "Daddy, who's it from?"

I looked at the signature on the card and instead of a name, it simply read: "From someone who loves you."

Our youngest girl, Laura piped up and said, "It's from God all right."

And it was.

These wonderful things have happened in the past seven years, but I want to add this: for about three years we went through some real tests, very much like wilderness living, where "manna" was provided day-by-day. More recently, it seems that we've come into Canaan, the promised land. For the last four years, God has blessed us financially in a remarkable way, proving that, "Where God guides, He provides."

He will not let us go under. Even though He
may not answer when we think He should, He
always answers soon enough.

But it hasn't been just the money, it's been
the ministry. I suppose I have seen a multipli-
cation of at least 500 percent in the effective-
ness of my ministry. I still minister much the
same way—teaching or preaching or sharing—
as I did back in the pastorate. That's because
I'm still the same person. But it's what God has
done that's amazing. When God leads, He puts
you where your ministry counts, and then He
multiplies the fruit of that ministry.

While I was still in the pastorate, I could
never have envisioned the places I would go, or
what I would do, or the things that would
happen. If I could have seen it all, I would have
rushed to get out. But God didn't reveal all the
details because He wanted me to walk by faith.
All these blessings have resulted, I believe, simply
because I started trusting God.

5

Now It's Your Turn

I believe it's clear to some of you by now that God wants you to take some fresh step of faith. I'm convinced He expects us all to commit ourselves to some additional degree. Do you want to see God directing your life more fully? What risk are you running now for Jesus' sake? What are you risking for Him that, if He doesn't come through with a miracle, you will go under? Remember, all progress in the Christian life is by faith.

The trouble with most of us is that we're not willing to crawl out on a limb, trusting God to hold us up as He has promised. I believe, in my case, when I surrendered my life to Christ in this deeper way, stepping out in faith, *I made God more responsible for me and my family than I had ever allowed Him to be before.* And He honored my decision and said, "Not only will I not let you go under, I'll bless your ministry in ways you never dreamed." And that's what He has done.

Although God won't divulge details ahead of
time, He has similar blessings in store for you.
If you're wondering why your life seems fruit-
less, why you aren't maturing in your faith,
instead of wondering, "How can I be sure it's
God?" ask yourself, "What risk am I running?"

I believe God is calling every one of you who
reads this to a deeper commitment: to begin to
trust God in a way where you will be sustained
by His power and not your own ability. As
long as you're doing only what *you* can do,
you get all the credit for it, and that's not
particularly pleasing to God. God isn't interested
in bringing credit to your name, He wants to
bring credit to the name of Jesus Christ. He
wants to put you into situations where *His*
miraculous power will provide the only solu-
tions, because then *He* gets the glory.

Every Christian needs to commit himself to
some ministry or venture where, if God doesn't
come through, he goes under. I believe that's
what God is calling you to do, even as He has
called me. It doesn't necessarily mean that you'll
change jobs, although it may. Or it might mean
some other radical course of action.

For many of you, I can tell you already what
it is that God wants you to do. It's that thing

He has already spoken to you about in your spirit, but when you hear Him say it, you reply, "Oh, no, God, not that!" You already know what He wants you to do, but you're frightened when you contemplate doing it. It's something He's calling you to do that you *can't* do without His help. Perhaps taking a new job in a different city, or opening your home for a prayer meeting, or witnessing to some obstinate neighbor. Perhaps making some sacrificial gift to a work the Lord has told you to support or even leaving secular employment to go "full time with the Lord." Whatever it is, God is calling you to commit yourself in a way that you haven't before, in order to depend more upon Him.

The thought may have been with you for weeks, months, or perhaps even years. But you've resisted, saying, "How can I be sure it's God?" Can you see now there's only one way you will *ever* be sure? That's to try it and see, remembering that as you begin to walk in faith, the Lord who loves you goes with you to close the wrong doors and open the right ones in order that His divine purpose may be accomplished in and through you.

Commit yourself that way, and God will honor your faith. He will pour forth His blessings, miracles, and provision in a way you've never seen. You can trust God to do that which He's promised, but first you must give Him the chance to release His miraculous power in your life, to bring glory—not to your name—but to His Son's name.

Don't be afraid. Trust Him. How will you ever know what He has in store for you unless you take the first step?

1   faith – –

2   God guides as we move,
            not all at start!

3   God has Goals – GOALS
          – – tests
          – – unpredictable
          – – in each venture

4.   God provides – –
        "where God guides,
            God provides"

      Examples of ~~each~~ above.

      God's power is not your ~~glory~~

MISTAKES ?
PROBLEMS ?